Down on the Farm

BEES

Sally Morgan

QED Publishing

QED

Copyright © QED Publishing 2007

First published in the UK in 2007 by
QED Publishing
A Quarto Group company
226 City Road
London EC1V 2TT
www.qed-publishing.co.uk

A catalogue record for this book is available
from the British Library.

ISBN 978 1 84538 807 2

Written by Sally Morgan
Designed by Tara Frese
Editor Corrine Ochiltree
Picture Researcher Nic Dean
Illustrations by Chris Davidson

Publisher Steve Evans
Creative Director Zeta Davies
Senior Editor Hannah Ray

Printed and bound in China

CONTENTS

Words in **bold** can be found in the Glossary on page 22.

Bees on the farm

Do you know where **honey** and **beeswax** come from? They are both made by busy, buzzing honeybees.

Honeybees are **insects**. They live in places where there are lots of flowers. Farmers and gardeners like bees because they carry **pollen** from one flower to another. This helps the flowers to make seeds.

Beekeepers keep their bees in beehives, like these.

Bees live together in groups called **colonies**. **Beekeepers** are people who look after bees. They build a **hive** for the bees to live in. Most beekeepers look after one or two hives, but some look after many more.

5

Bees from top to tail

There are three types of honeybee that live in a hive. Most are **worker bees**. These are the bees you see buzzing between flowers. A worker bee has a hairy body around 1–1.5cm long. They have two pairs of see-through wings and an orange and black striped body.

Wings

Hairy body

Eye

Sting

Legs

Antenna

This large queen bee is surrounded by worker bees.

Height of a six-year-old child   Height of a beehive

FARM FACT
A honeybee can sting. However, once it has used its sting, the bee dies.

The largest bee in a hive is the **queen** bee. There is only one queen bee in each hive and she is in charge. Male honeybees are called **drones**. There are hundreds of drones living in each hive.

7

It's a bee's life...

The queen bee lays her eggs in the hive. After three days, an egg hatches into a **larva**. The larva is white and has no wings. Worker bees feed the larva with bee bread. This is a mixture of honey and pollen.

Larvae look a bit like wiggly maggots.

After four days, the larva turns into a **pupa**. It stops moving while its body changes into an adult bee.

8

This baby bee used to be a larva.

Some larvae are given special food to eat, called royal jelly. The worker bees make it in their mouths. Larvae who are fed royal jelly turn into new queens.

Most worker bees live for about six to seven weeks. Drones live for about two months. A queen bee can live for up to two years.

Flower friends

Each day, honeybees leave the hive and fly around looking for flowers. They drink the sugary **nectar** made by many flowers.

Flowers produce pollen, too. This looks like yellow dust. Bees put the pollen into special baskets on their legs. They then take the pollen and nectar back to their hive.

This honeybee has collected lots of pollen in its leg basket.

FARM FACT
Bees carry the nectar they collect in a special nectar stomach. They have to visit as many as 1500 flowers to fill their honey stomach.

Bees are very helpful little insects because they help to make flowers grow. They carry pollen from one flower to another. This is important because the pollen is needed by the flowers to make their seeds, from which new flowers grow.

Yummy honey

Worker bees chew the nectar and pollen to make it into honey. Honey is very sweet because it is made up of sugar. Bees eat some honey and beekeepers collect the rest. It is strained to remove any beeswax and put into jars to sell.

As much as 70kg of honey can be collected from one hive in a year. That's about the same weight as a grown-up man!

This beekeeper is removing a comb from the hive.

12

FARM FACT
Honey can be used to treat wounds. It stops germs getting into the wound and helps it to heal more quickly.

Honey varies in colour from almost black to white. It can have a strong or a mild taste. It all depends on the types of flowers the bees have visited. Honey made from heather flowers has a smoky taste.

Living in a hive

As many as 50 000 honeybees may live in a hive at a time. That's a lot of bees! Inside the hive, the bees use beeswax to build a **comb**. Each comb is made up of thousands of tiny, six-sided holes, called cells.

When they check their hives, beekeepers wear special clothes so they do not get stung.

In summer, the beekeepers move the hives so the bees have lots of flowers to visit. At the end of summer, they remove some of the combs to collect the honey that has been stored inside. In winter months, when there are few flowers, the beekeepers feed the bees a sugary food, called candy.

15

Bees around the world

KILLER HONEYBEES

The Africanized honeybee is a cross between the honeybee from Europe and the African honeybee. It is found in South America. It has been nicknamed the killer bee because it is a fierce bee that will chase a person more than 100m to sting them. Run!

GIANT HONEYBEE

This wild bee is found in Asia and grows up to 15mm long. It makes its nest in trees and on cliffs. Beekeepers don't keep it because it is not very friendly. It will sting a person without reason.

DWARF HONEYBEE

This mini bee is only 8mm long. That's tiny! It lives in southern parts of Asia and is a wild type of bee. Instead of living in a hive, this honeybee attaches its combs to tree branches.

Bee customs

ANCIENT EGYPT

Honey was very valuable in Ancient Egypt. It was used like money. One hundred pots of honey were enough to buy an ox or a donkey.

GREECE

In Greece it used to be **traditional** for a bride to dip her finger into a pot of honey and make a sign of the cross before entering her new home. People believed it would bring the bride good luck.

ALL OVER THE WORLD

In many parts of the world, honey is part of the Jewish New Year celebrations. Part of the celebration involves dipping slices of apple into honey. This brings good luck for the coming year.

Make a buzzy bee

Making your own honeybee is great fun and very easy. All you need is an egg box, scissors, masking tape, paints and paintbrush, pipe cleaners, glue, sticky tape and a plant stick.

1 Cut out two egg shapes from the egg box and stick them together with tape to make an oval shape.

2 Paint the body of the bee. Don't forget that bees have stripy bodies!

3 Cut out a small circle from the egg box and stick it on the front of your bee to make the head. Use your paints to paint on big, boggly eyes.

4 Cut short lengths of pipe cleaner. Stick them onto your bee to make legs and antennae. Bend two more pipe cleaners to make wings, and stick them onto your bee.

5 Make a small hole in the underside of the bee and push the stick into it. Pop your bee in a vase of flowers.

Glossary and Index

antenna (plural antennae) feelers on an insect's body that it uses to touch and feel things

beekeeper a person who looks after bees

beeswax a waxy substance made by bees

colonies large groups of bees that live together

comb a place where honeybees store honey in a beehive

drone the name given to a male honeybee

hive the place where honeybees live

honey a sugary substance made by bees

insects small animals with six legs and wings

larva (plural larvae) the name given to the young of an insect. A larva hatches from an egg

nectar the sugary liquid made by some flowers

pollen the yellow 'dust' made by a flower

pupa the stage in the life of an insect in which the body of the larva changes into the adult insect

queen the female honeybee that lays eggs

traditional a custom or way of doing something that is passed from parent to child

worker bees a type of bee that lives in the hive and collects nectar and pollen from flowers

23

Ideas for teachers and parents

- Watch honeybees at work in a garden or park. Make a note of the flowers the bees visit. Watch how the bees work their way around a flower. Take care that the children do not get too close to the bees, so they do not get stung!

- Look for some interesting recipes that use honey. Make them with the children, then see what they taste like.

- Ask a local beekeeper if it is possible to see inside a hive. Often, local beekeeper associations have open days for members of the public.

- Make a collage of honeybees. Take a large piece of white paper and draw outlines of bees on it, along with some flowers. Look through old magazines and cut out any pictures of bees and flowers. Stick these on the outline to make a colourful collage.

- Make a wordsearch using the bee-related vocabulary in this book.

- Encourage the children to think up jokes and stories about bees. See if they can write a poem or a short story about a honeybee.

- Carry out a simple experiment to see which colours bees prefer. Place three small circles of coloured card (red, yellow and blue) on the ground near a flowerbed and place a little sugar water in the middle of each circle. Stand back and watch which colour of card the bees prefer.

- There are many different types of honey on sale in the shops. Ask the children to look at the labels to see what type of flowers were used by the bees to make their honey. Some are made by bees visiting one type of flower, for example, heather or lavender. It is also possible to buy honey made by rainforest bees. Buy a couple of the different types of honey and do a taste test with the children.

PLEASE NOTE

• Check that each child does not have any food intolerances before carrying out the honey recipes and the taste test.